NAILED IT!

Extreme

SKATE-
BOARDING

Virginia Loh-Hagan

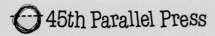

45th Parallel Press

Published in the United States of America by Cherry Lake Publishing
Ann Arbor, Michigan
www.cherrylakepublishing.com

Content Adviser: Liv Williams, Editor, www.iLivExtreme.com
Reading Adviser: Marla Conn, ReadAbility, Inc.
Photo Credits: ©Maxim Blinkov/Shutterstock.com, cover, 1; ©A.Richardo/Shutterstock.com, 5; ©Cdrin/Shutterstock.com, 6; ©Blulz60/istockphoto.com, 9; ©DAN HIMBRECHTS/EPA/Newscom, 11; ©Frenzel/Shutterstock.com, 12; ©REUTERS/China Newsphoto/Landov, 15; ©Purestock/Thinkstock.com, 17; ©Paul Topp/Dreamstime.com, 19; ©lzf/Shutterstock.com, 21; ©Tommaso79/Dreamstime.com, 22; ©Charles Knox/Shutterstock.com, 25; ©Tamara Hughbanks/Dreamstime.com, 27; ©ARENA Creative/Shutterstock.com, 29; ©Trusjom/Shutterstock.com, multiple interior pages; ©Kues/Shutterstock.com, multiple interior pages

45th Parallel Press is an imprint of Cherry Lake Publishing.

Library of Congress Cataloging-in-Publication Data

Loh-Hagan, Virginia.
  Extreme skateboarding / Virginia Loh-Hagan.
    pages cm. -- (Nailed It!)
  Includes bibliographical references and index.
  ISBN 978-1-63470-015-3 (hardcover) -- ISBN 978-1-63470-069-6 (pdf) -- ISBN 978-1-63470-042-9 (paperback) -- ISBN 978-1-63470-096-2 (ebook)
  1. Skateboarding--Juvenile literature. 2. Extreme sports--Juvenile literature. 3. ESPN X-Games--Juvenile literature. I. Title.

GV859.8.L65 2015
796.22--dc23

                    2015006304

ABOUT THE AUTHOR

Dr. Virginia Loh-Hagan is an author, university professor, former classroom teacher, and curriculum designer. After watching *Gleaming the Cube,* she crushed on Christian Slater. She lives in San Diego with her very tall husband and very naughty dogs. To learn more about her, visit www.virginialoh.com.

Table of Contents

About the Author 2

CHAPTER 1:
Falling, Failing, and Flying 4
CHAPTER 2:
No Guts, No Glory! No Limits! 10
CHAPTER 3:
From Surfing Waves to Sidewalks 16
CHAPTER 4:
Rebels with a Cause 20
CHAPTER 5:
Skate and Create! 26

Did You Know? 30

Consider This! 31

Learn More 31

Glossary 32

Index 32

Falling, Failing, and Flying

Why is Jake Brown a good example of an extreme skateboarder? What are the Summer X Games? What are the goals of extreme skateboarders? What risks do they take?

Jake Brown takes an elevator. He goes to the top of the **MegaRamp**. He goes down the huge ramp. He gets speed. He goes up the **slope**, or curve. He jumps across the giant gap. He makes two circles in the air. He doesn't grab his board. This trick is called a 720. He's the first person to do it.

Brown lands on the **quarterpipe**. A quarterpipe is half of a U-shaped ramp. He goes down the slope. He speeds up the other slope. He's in the air. Then he loses control of his skateboard. He falls more than 45 feet (13.7 meters). He hits the ground hard. His shoes fly off his feet. He's still for eight minutes.

Brown finally wakes up. He asks, "Did I make the 720?" Brown is an extreme skateboarder. He lives for skating.

The MegaRamp is a huge skate structure. It consists of the roll-in ramp, the gap jump, and the quarterpipe ramp.

Skateboarders should remember not to catch themselves with their hands when they fall.

Advice from the Field: How to Fall

How did Jake Brown survive? He was falling headfirst. He moved so his feet were facing down instead. He spread out the impact of his crash between his ankle, knee, and hip. If he were spinning or somersaulting, he wouldn't have been able to control how he landed. His helmet prevented a deadly head injury.

Tips for falling:

☞ Roll on your shoulder or back. This evenly spreads out the impact.

☞ Do **NOT** catch yourself with your hands.

☞ Fall on your knees when on ramps. (Kneepads protect knees.) Then slide down the ramp.

He was lucky to be alive. He hurt many body parts. He got better. He started skating again. He practiced. He trained.

Brown participates in the Summer X Games. The X Games are a **competition**, or contest. They are for extreme sports. He does crazy tricks in the air. He won a gold medal. He won two years in a row.

Danny Way invented the MegaRamp. He respects Jake Brown. He said, "It's not about how hard he can fall. He's one of the guys out there that's **innovating**." Skaters invent. They make changes. They push skateboarding to the next level.

Skaters take big risks. Their main goal is flying, or catching big air. To do that, they must fall and fail. Tony Hawk landed a 900. He was the first person to do it. A 900 is two and a half turns. He failed 10 times before landing it. Gabriel Ramos tried to land a 1080. A 1080 is three turns. He failed 29 times.

"It's not about how hard he can fall. He's one of the guys out there that's innovating."

Extreme skateboarders fall many times before they catch air.

No Guts, No Glory! No Limits!

What makes extreme skateboarding extreme? How do skaters get air? What are the three styles of extreme skateboarding?

Difficult tricks make skateboarding extreme. To get air, they use or invent **obstacles**. Obstacles are skating structures. They can be ramps. They can be things like benches or stairs. William Spencer did front flips down a set of stairs. Then he landed on his board. Adam Miller skated down a ramp. His board hit another board. He did backflips over six stairs. Then he landed on the other board. Skaters are always creating new tricks.

There are three styles of extreme skateboarding. First, there is **vertical** or **vert** skateboarding. Vert skaters use obstacles to build speed. They get vertical, or straight up, in the air. They do spins. They also do **aerials**. Aerials are tricks in the air. Tony Hawk has created many vert tricks.

Tony Hawk is called the "Birdman." He looks like he's flying when he's skating.

Extreme skateboarders do a lot of different tricks.

The second type is street skateboarding. Street skaters skate on railings, curbs, and stairs. They skate on sidewalks too. There are two types of street skaters. **Technical** skaters need special skills. They do fancy combinations of moves. And stunt skaters do risky tricks. They use speed and height. Chad Muska likes stunts. He jumps over many sets of stairs.

The third type is freestyling. Freestyle skaters skate on flat ground. They skate in parking lots or basketball courts.

When Extreme Is Too Extreme!

The "Broadway Bomb" started in 2002. It's an unofficial and unsafe 8-mile (12.8 km) street race. It takes place in busy Manhattan city traffic. There is no security. It grew from 16 racers to over 2,000. In 2012, the race was declared illegal, or not allowed by law. It was canceled. But skaters still showed up. In 2013, 38 arrests were made. The youngest people arrested were 13 years old. A skater said, "I don't want to get arrested, but we ride skateboards ... It's skateboarding and fun."

They do balance and flip tricks. Mark Gonzales is the "father of street skating." He said he doesn't need parks and ramps. He can skate "rad" anywhere.

Some stunts are too extreme for the X Games. Danny Way jumped out of a helicopter. He jumped 18 feet and 3 inches (5.5 m) above a ramp. He called it the Bomb Drop. He did another famous stunt. He jumped over the Great Wall of China. He was the first skater to do this.

Bob Burnquist skated down a 40-foot (12 m) ramp. He sped up a 40-foot rail. Then he dropped 1,600 feet (487.6 m) into the Grand Canyon!

Skaters need balance, strength, and timing.

They also need guts.

"Skaters need balance, strength, and timing."

Danny Way jumped over the Great Wall of China five times!

From Surfing Waves to Sidewalks

What are the three main parts of a skateboard? How did skateboarding develop?

Extreme skateboarders don't see a wooden board on wheels. They see a new way to fly.

There are three main parts of a skateboard. The **deck** is the board. This is the first part. **Kicktails** are the tips of the deck. The front kicktail is called the **nose**. The rear is called the **tail**. The **trucks** are the wheel axles. Trucks are the second part. The wheels are the third main part.

Skateboarding started in California. In the 1950s, surfing was popular. Sometimes the waves were too calm to ride.

Bored surfers got creative. They figured out how to surf on land. Bill Richards and his son, Mark, were surfers. They used the wheels of roller skates and scooters. They attached these wheels to wooden boards. The boards were called "sidewalk surfers."

These early skateboards were unsafe. Skaters couldn't do tricks on them. The boards were slow and heavy.

The coolest thing about skateboards is all the different designs.

Extreme Skateboarding: Know the Lingo

Air: lifting off the ground using body weight and momentum

Bail: pulling out of a trick to avoid wiping out

Barge: skating in places where it is not allowed

Carve: taking long wide turns

Fakie: riding backward

Gnarly: beyond rad, beyond extreme, perfection; dangerous

Goofy: left foot on the tail, right foot on the nose

Grab: holding the deck while flying through the air

Grind: scraping the trucks along an obstacle

Rad: cool, radical

Run: series of tricks and combinations, continuous skating time

Shred: hard, fast skateboarding

Slide: skidding over an obstacle using the deck

Stall: stopping the skateboard by balancing on the tail or trucks

Stoked: excited and pleased

Wheelie: balancing on the front or back wheels while riding

Surfing had a huge impact on skateboarding.

The wheels were metal or clay. This made the skateboard hard to control. Skaters hurt themselves.

Skaters do dangerous things. But they're not dumb. They make sure they have the correct skills and gear.

Rebels with a Cause

What are four major changes that improved skateboarding? Who created these changes?

Skaters **improve** their gear and the sport. They make things better.

Four people changed skateboarding. The first change happened in the 1970s. Frank Nasworthy invented **urethane** wheels. Urethane is like a rubbery plastic. These new wheels made skateboards safer. They gave skaters better grip. They lasted longer. They made less noise.

This led to other improvements. Trucks were invented. Boards got lighter and faster. This means skaters could skate almost anywhere.

Second, the Z-Boys of Dogtown introduced a new style. They were a professional skating team. They skated **aggressively**, or fiercely. They skated low to the ground. They touched the ground like surfers touch the waves. They competed in contests. They were **rebels**, or rule-breakers. All skaters wanted to be like them.

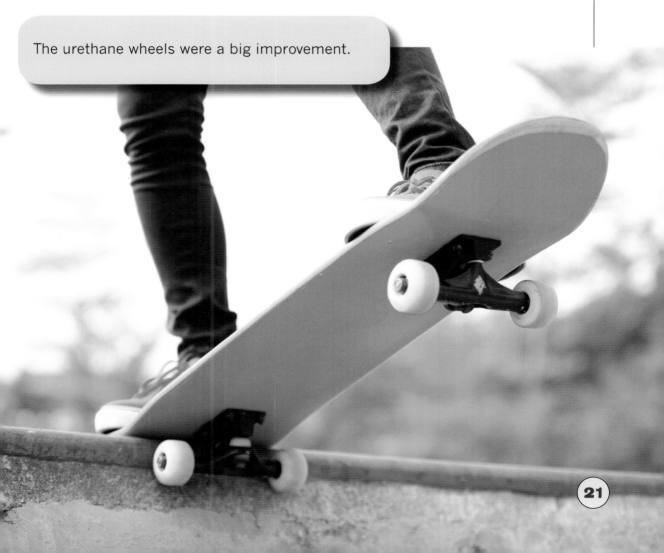

The urethane wheels were a big improvement.

The Z-Boys were some of the first skaters to skate in empty pools.

The third change happened in the 1970s. California was having a dry season. Water was limited. So people didn't fill their swimming pools. Skaters practiced in these empty pools.

NAILED IT!

Spotlight Biography: Peggy Oki

Not all the Z-Boys were boys. Peggy Oki was the only girl on the team. She liked surfing, motocross, and skateboarding. Oki started skating at 10 years old. She competed at the Del Mar Nationals in 1975. Her performance was questioned because she "skated like a guy." The girls she skated against said it wasn't fair. But a judge said she was better than the guys too. Soon after this contest, she stopped competing. She said, "It wasn't always about the best skater, and it wasn't fun for me to hang around all day, hardly actually skating." She is in the Skateboarding Hall of Fame. Today, she still skates. She is an artist and an environmental activist.

Tony Alva was a Z-Boy. One day, he flew off a pool edge. This was the first aerial. At the same time, Tom Stewart invented the **half-pipe**. The half-pipe is a U-shaped ramp. Vertical skateboarding was born.

Alan "Ollie" Gelfand invented the fourth change. He was 13 years old. He invented a trick. It was called the "ollie." He popped his skateboard. It went into the air. His feet stayed on the board. This move changed how people skated. Most tricks are based on this move. Skaters no longer needed ramps to catch air.

Extreme skateboarding is a new sport. Young people created it for young people.

"Vertical skatingboarding was born."

The "ollie" is an important move. Skaters can get air without an obstacle.

Skate and Create!

What are some challenges skaters face? Why was skateboarding good for Tony Hawk? What other sports are influenced by skateboarding?

Some cities **ban** skateboarding. These cities do not allow it. Skating can destroy city property. City officials want skaters off the streets. Some cities have skateboard parks. Parks with vertical ramps are expensive. Many had to close. This did not stop skaters. They found places to skate.

Skaters fight against a bad image. Each year, 50,000 skaters are sent to hospitals. The California Medical Association called skateboarding a "new medical **menace**." A menace is a problem. Football causes more injuries. But skateboarding is connected to rebels.

Skaters mentor each other. Stacy Peralta was a Z-Boy. He formed his own professional skating team. It was called the Bones Brigade. A brigade is a gang. This group introduced Tony Hawk to skateboarding. It was perfect for Tony. He had trouble following rules. He was easily distracted. He was skinny. He was teased. He wore elbow pads on his knees. Skateboarding gave Tony a chance to do his own thing.

These No Skateboarding signs are common in many cities. Wentzle Ruml was a Z-Boy. He said, "This is concrete warfare."

NO SKATEBOARDS ALLOWED

Extreme skateboarding is important to extreme sports. Its moves and attitudes influenced other sports. These sports include snowboarding, BMX freestyle, and kite surfing. And more. Skating is about innovating. It is about inventing. Its motto is "Skate and create."

That Happened?!?

Jon Comer is a professional amputee skater. An amputee is a person who has had an arm or leg cut off. When he was 4 years old, Comer was playing in an alley. A teenage driver ran over his leg and fled the scene. Neighbors lifted the car off Comer's leg. His leg was cut off from the knee down. He has a "fake leg." He followed his older brother around at the skate parks. He loved it! He started skating at age 10. In his first contest, he lost his balance. A rope caught his leg. His fake leg went flying. The crowd was scared. They thought Jon's leg had been ripped off.

The world of extreme sports owes much to the "do your own thing" attitude of extreme skateboarding.

Did You Know?

- Tony Hawk and Andy Macdonald skateboarded in the White House.

- California is the skateboard capital of the world. San Diego is home to many great skateboarders, including Jake Brown, Bob Burnquist, Tony Hawk, and Shaun White. Bob Burnquist has one of the three existing MegaRamps in his backyard.

- Andy Macdonald wanted to get better at skateboarding. So he moved from cold Boston to sunny San Diego. He worked at SeaWorld. He wore the Shamu costume. In 1999, Macdonald set the record for longest jump on a skateboard. He jumped 52 feet and 10 inches (16 m). He jumped over four parked cars.

- The Z-Boys' last skating sessions were at the "Dogbowl." Dino was one of their skating friends. He was dying of brain cancer. Dino asked his father to drain their pool. He wanted the Z-Boys to skate in it. Dogs were always hanging around. So they called it the Dogbowl.

- Even dogs can catch air! Extreme Pete is a Jack Russell terrier. He can do the half-pipe. He can also ride a skateboard down stairs. Bulldogs are especially good at skateboarding. They are low to the ground and have a wide body.

- A goat in Fort Myers, Florida, set a world record. He achieved "farthest distance skateboarding by a goat." The goat traveled 118 feet (36 m).

Consider This!

TAKE A POSITION! Some extreme skateboarders reject sponsorships and competitions. They think to be extreme means to go against the mainstream. Accepting sponsorships and competing means following rules. But sponsorships and competitions allow extreme athletes to do what they love. They also promote the activities. Where do you stand on this issue? Do you think sponsorships and competitions are good or bad for skateboarding? Argue your point with reasons and evidence.

SAY WHAT? June 21 is "Go Skateboarding Day." Learn more about it. Explain how people celebrate this day. Explain how this day celebrates skateboarding.

THINK ABOUT IT! Skip Englblom was the co-owner of the Zephyr skateboard company. They formed the Z-Boys. Englblom said, "Children took the ruins of the 20th century and made art of it." Craig Stecyk wrote articles about the Z-Boys. He said, "Skaters by their very nature are urban guerrillas." Urban means city. Guerrillas are soldiers fighting for a cause. What do these quotations mean to you?

SEE A DIFFERENT SIDE! Skateboarding has caused injuries and deaths. It has also caused destruction of public property. Street skaters have hurt walkers. They have caused car accidents. Imagine you are a parent or a city official. How would you view skateboarding? What are the issues from either perspective?

Learn More: Resources

Primary Sources

Dogtown and Z-Boys (2001), a documentary directed by Stacy Peralta, written by Stacy Peralta and Craig Stecyk.

Tony Hawk: Professional Skateboarder by Tony Hawk with Sean Mortimer (It Books, 2002).

Secondary Sources

Crossingham, John, and Bobbie Kalman. *Extreme Skateboarding.* New York: Crabtree Publishing Company, 2004.

Sandler, Michael. *Gnarly Skateboarders.* New York: Bearport Publishing, 2010.

Web Sites

Exploratorium—Skateboard Science: www.exploratorium.edu/skateboarding/

Skate Park Association International: www.spausa.org

X Games—Skateboarding: http://xgames.espn.go.com/skateboarding/

Glossary

aerials (AIR-ee-uhlz) tricks in the air

aggressively (uh-GRES-iv-lee) fiercely, hard and tough

ban (BAN) do not allow by law, make illegal

competition (kahm-puh-TISH-uhn) contest

deck (DEK) actual board or body of a skateboard

half-pipe (HAF-pipe) large U-shaped ramps used in gravity extreme sports; also called verticals or verts

improve (im-PROOV) to make better

innovating (IN-oh-vay-ting) creating, inventing

kicktails (KIK-taylz) tips of the deck

MegaRamp (MEG-uh-ramp) a large skate structure with a roll-in ramp, the gap jump, and the final quarterpipe ramp

menace (MEN-uhs) annoying problem

nose (NOZE) front kicktail of the skateboard

obstacles (OB-stuh-kuhlz) things skaters can skate or grind on

rebels (REB-uhlz) rule-breakers

quarterpipe (KWOR-tuhr-pipe) half of a U-shaped ramp, a quarter section of a pipe

slope (SLOHP) downward curved skate structure

tail (TAYL) rear kicktail of skateboard

technical (TEK-nih-kuhl) requiring special skills or techniques

trucks (TRUKS) wheel axles

urethane (YUR-uh-thane) rubbery plastic that skateboard wheels are made of

vertical (VUR-tih-kuhl) or **vert** (VURT) getting high up or straight up in the air

Index

aerials, 11, 24

amputee, 28

Broadway Bomb, 13

catching air, 8, 9, 10, 24, 25

challenges, 26–27

extreme skateboarding styles of, 10–13, 21

falling, 6, 7, 8, 9

freestyling, 13

gear, 20

half-pipe, 24, 30

injuries, 5, 7, 26–27

lingo, 18

MegaRamp, 4, 5, 8, 30

900, 8

ollie, 24, 25

quarterpipe, 4

risks, 8, 720, 4–5

skateboards, 16–17, 19, 21

street skateboarding, 11–12

stunt skaters, 12, 14–15

surfing, 16–17, 19

swimming pools, 22, 23–24, 30

technical skating, 12 1080, 8

tricks, 10, 24

vertical skateboarding, 10–11, 24

wheels, 20, 21

Z-Boys, 21, 22, 23, 24, 27, 30